LAUNCH PAD
LIBRARY

ANIMAL
HOMES

ANITA GANERI

STAMPLEY

How to use this book

Cross-references
Above some of the chapter titles, you will find a list of other chapters in the book that are related to the topic. Turn to these pages to find out more about each subject.

See for yourself
See-for-yourself bubbles give you the chance to test out some of the ideas in this book. They explain what you will need and what you have to do to see if an idea really works.

Quiz corner
In the quiz corner, you will find a list of questions. The answers to the quiz questions are somewhere in the same chapter. Try to answer all the questions about each subject.

Chatterboxes
Chatterboxes give you interesting facts about other things that are related to the subject.

Glossary
Difficult words are explained in the glossary on page 31. These words are in **bold** type in the book. Look them up in the glossary to find out what they mean.

Index
The index is on page 32. It is a list of important words mentioned in the book, with page numbers next to the entries. If you want to read about a subject, look it up in the index, then turn to the page number given.

Contents

Choosing a Home

Animals live in all kinds of homes, from dusty holes in the ground to grass nests woven in trees. Animals need homes where they can sleep, shelter from harsh weather, raise their young, and hide from enemies. Each home has to be just right for the animal that lives there.

Homes everywhere
Animals make their homes in a variety of places. Many birds build nests in the treetops, while insects shelter under leaves and in cracks in tree trunks. Other animals make their homes in dark caves, in holes underground, or underwater.

▲ Wildebeest and zebras have no fixed homes. They live in large **herds** and roam the grasslands of Africa, stopping where they find food and water.

▼ In Central America, oropendola birds build long, hanging nests in trees.

Making a home
Animals have different ways of making homes. They build, dig, drill, and sew. Some animals use materials that they make in their bodies, such as wax. Most animals use things that they find around them, such as stones, leaves, and mud. In spring, look for birds collecting twigs to make their nests.

▲ The harvest mouse weaves its home out of grass. It uses the nest to care for its young.

Quiz Corner

● Why do animals need homes?

● For what does the harvest mouse use its nest?

● Do zebras have a fixed home?

● Name four materials that animals use to make their homes.

Look at: Tree Homes, page 12

Caves and Dens

Caves make warm, safe homes for all kinds of animals. Many animals live in caves in the sides of cliffs or mountains. Others make their own caves by digging snug holes in the ground or in snow. These holes are often called dens.

Bear's den

There are many kinds of bears, including brown, grizzly, and polar bears. Most bears live in caves, in holes in the ground, or in hollow trees, but polar bears dig their dens in the snow. Some bears stay inside their caves or dens all winter.

▶ During the day, bats sleep in caves. There they are safe from **predators**, such as snakes, rats, and owls.

◀ Grizzly bear cubs are born in a den in late winter. In spring, the mother and cubs go outside because they need to find food.

Bat caves

A cave may be home to thousands of bats. They sleep there during the day, then fly off at night to search for food. Bats also use their caves as **nurseries**. The baby bats cling to the cave roof and walls while their mothers go hunting.

Winter sleep

In winter, the weather is cold and there is little food to eat. Animals such as bats and bears save their **energy** by sleeping in their caves until spring. This long sleep is called hibernation.

*Bats hang upside down to rest.
They cling to the roofs of caves
with their clawed toes.*

*To keep warm, bats fold their
wings around their bodies
and huddle close together.*

CHATTERBOX

An Asian bird called
a cave swiftlet makes
its nest in a cave.
It uses its own spit,
or saliva, to make
a cup-shaped nest.
People collect the
nests to make soup.

Quiz Corner

- Why do caves make good homes?

- Which kind of bear makes its den in the snow?

- How do bats keep warm while they rest?

Look at: Underwater Homes, page 24

Beaver Lodges

Beavers are master builders. A beaver family will work together to build its home, called a lodge. They cut down wood and pile it up with mud and stones to make a barrier, or **dam**, across a river. The dam holds back the water and makes a lake. Then the beavers build their lodge in the middle of the lake, safe from **predators**.

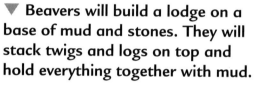

▼ Beavers will build a lodge on a base of mud and stones. They will stack twigs and logs on top and hold everything together with mud.

▲ Beavers eat bark which they strip from twigs with their sharp front teeth.

Other beavers may build on the lake, too.

8

Living quarters

Beavers hollow out the middle of the lodge to make a room where they will live. The room is above the water level, so it is warm and dry. Young beavers, called kits, are born there. They live with their parents for two years, then they leave to make their own lodges.

Repairing the dam

Beavers work hard to keep the dam in good repair. They patch up gaps with mud and sticks to keep the water from seeping through. This keeps the level of the lake high and hides the secret underwater entrances to the lodge.

Beavers leave gaps between the sticks so that the lodge has plenty of air.

A thick layer of mud keeps heat in and water out.

An underwater tunnel leads into the lodge.

CHATTERBOX

Like beavers, people build dams to make lakes. Instead of sticks and stones, people use concrete to hold back riverwater. The water from the lakes is used to water fields and to make drinking water.

Food stores

In winter, beavers need a supply of bark to eat. The cold lake water makes the perfect storage area. In autumn, the beavers cut down branches and sink them into the lake. The water acts like a refrigerator, keeping the bark fresh.

Quiz Corner

- What do beavers use to make their dams and lodges?
- What do beavers use to cut branches?
- How do beavers get in and out of the lodge?

Termite Towers

Tiny insects called termites build some of the most amazing homes. One termite is only as big as a grain of rice, but together millions of them can build a nest three times taller than an adult human. Each nest contains a king and queen termite, who spend most of their lives **breeding**. The other termites help build the nest, find food, and care for the young.

Mud walls

Termites called workers build the nest from mud. When the walls dry, they set as hard as rock. These strong walls help to protect the nest from attack by **predators**, such as anteaters and chimpanzees.

Inside a tower

There are many rooms in the nest. In some rooms the termites raise their young, while in others they grow **fungus** and store wood to eat. The king and queen live in the largest room, the royal chamber.

long tunnels help cool the nest

food stores

fungus garden

nurseries

royal chamber

▲ When termites fly off to make a new nest, other animals, such as this family of dwarf mongooses, move in.

Keeping cool
Air inside the nest can become hot and stuffy, so the termites have a clever air-conditioning system. They make long tunnels that let warm air escape from the nest and let cold air seep in. The termites also coat the walls of their home with water or spit to keep it cool.

◀ This termite nest is in Australia. It can take up to 50 years to build a nest this size.

Quiz Corner

● From what are termite nests made?

● Name two animals that like to eat termites.

● Where do the king and queen termite live?

Look at: Beehives, page 14; Birds' Nests, page 16; Other Kinds of Nests, page 18

Tree Homes

Trees are home to animals of all shapes and sizes. Birds and small **mammals** rest on branches high above the ground or in holes in the tree trunk. Wood lice, spiders, and beetles hide in cracks in the bark, while moths and butterflies make homes for their eggs among the leaves.

▼ The squirrel makes its round home, called a drey, from twigs and leaves.

The squirrel lines its drey with moss and bark.

▲ Plants called bromeliads grow on rain forest trees. When it rains, bromeliads fill with water and make homes for tree frogs.

Leafy homes

Many creatures use leaves for shelter. The squirrel covers its drey with leaves to hide it from other animals. In Central America, tiny tent-making bats snuggle in groups underneath palm leaves, safe from heavy rain.

Under the roots

Badgers often make their homes, called sets, underneath tree roots. There the soil is usually dry and easy to dig. The roots help to keep the set from collapsing.

CHATTERBOX

Tailor ants sew leaves into nests, but they don't use needles and thread. They take their own grubs, which are the baby stage of an ant, and run them between the leaf edges. The grubs spit out a sticky silk, which glues the leaves together.

In the trunk

When a branch falls off a tree, it often leaves a hole in the trunk. These holes make ideal nesting places for many birds. Some birds make their own nest holes. The woodpecker takes about two weeks to peck out a hole. Its extra-strong skull protects its head while it pecks.

Quiz Corner

- Where do tent-making bats live?

- What do tailor ants use to sew leaves into nests?

- How long does it take a woodpecker to make its nest?

▲ The woodpecker feeds its chicks on insects and grubs.

Look at: Other Kinds of Nests, page 18

Beehives

Honeybees live in large, busy groups. They build their homes, called hives, in hollow trees. Bees make wax inside their bodies. They shape the wax with their legs and jaws into six-sided pockets, or cells. Bees connect rows of cells to make a **honeycomb**. There are many honeycombs in one hive.

▲ People build hives specially for bees. They take care of the bees and harvest some of the honey that the bees make.

Smart builders
Bees build their homes carefully as a team. All the wax cells are the same size and shape. Some cells are used for storing honey and **pollen** to feed the bee grubs when they hatch. Other cells contain eggs laid by the largest bee, called the queen bee.

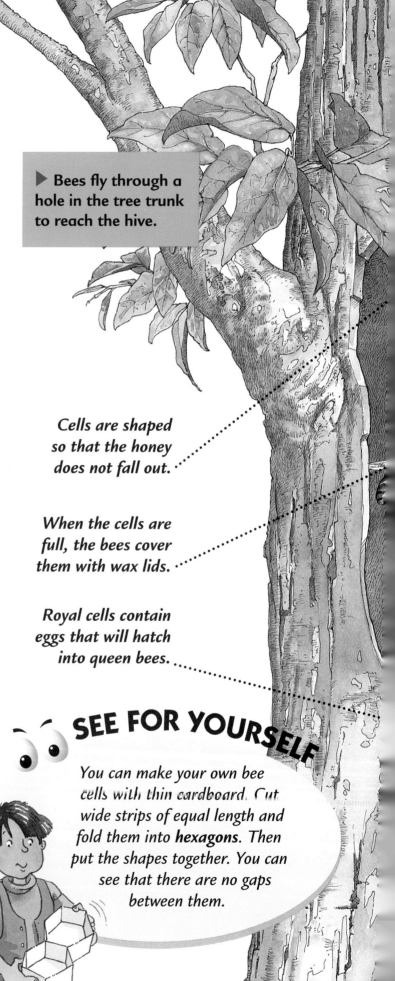

▶ Bees fly through a hole in the tree trunk to reach the hive.

Cells are shaped so that the honey does not fall out.

When the cells are full, the bees cover them with wax lids.

Royal cells contain eggs that will hatch into queen bees.

SEE FOR YOURSELF

*You can make your own bee cells with thin cardboard. Cut wide strips of equal length and fold them into **hexagons**. Then put the shapes together. You can see that there are no gaps between them.*

Bees called workers carry pollen to the hive on their back legs.

The queen bee is in charge of the other bees.

Larvae live in some of the cells.

Quiz Corner

- What parts of a bee's body are used to shape wax?

- Why do people keep bees?

- What is stored inside the cells of a hive?

Look at: Choosing a Home, page 4; Caves and Dens, page 6; Tree Homes, page 12

Birds' Nests

The type of animal home you probably know best is a bird's nest. This is where birds lay their eggs and raise their young. Birds build nests with materials that they find nearby, such as grass, animal fur, mud, or seaweed. Some nests are simple twig platforms, while others are cups lined with feathers or petals.

▲ The reed warbler weaves a small grass nest and ties it to the surrounding reeds.

Building sites

Many birds build their nests in trees or bushes, but any safe place will do. The kingfisher digs a tunnel in a riverbank. At the end of the tunnel it puts a nesting chamber. There, the kingfisher lays its eggs on a cushion of fish bones and scales.

Weaving skills

The weaver bird builds its nest by knotting and weaving grass. Using its beak and feet, it ties blades of grass to a branch to make a ring. Then the bird weaves more grass into the ring to make a ball. Finally, it adds a long entrance tunnel, which makes the nest hard for snakes to enter and steal the eggs.

Great and small

Nests come in all shapes and sizes. The reed warbler builds a tightly woven nest about the size of a small mug. At its full size, an eagle's nest can be as wide as a car.

CHATTERBOX

Flamingos live in large, shallow lakes. They build their nests from mud, which they scoop up from the bottom of the lake. The top of each nest is shaped like a cup to keep their eggs from rolling into the water.

Quiz Corner

- Where do kingfishers make their nests?

- Name three materials that birds use to build their nests.

- What keeps a flamingo's egg from rolling off its nest?

◄ Eagles build their nests in treetops or high up on cliff ledges. An eagle's nest is called an eyrie.

Look at: Tree Homes, page 12

Other Kinds of Nests

Birds are not the only animals that build nests. Many animals live in nests made from all kinds of materials, including paper, sand, and mud. Some animals live in nests all year round, while others make nests when they need to lay eggs.

Paper homes
Some wasps live in groups and build their nests out of paper. The female wasp makes paper by chewing plants or pieces of old wood. She spreads the paper in layers to build pockets, or cells, similar to those built by bees. The cells are used for **nurseries** and food storage.

▶ Wasps hang paper nests from trees or grasses, or they build them in empty **burrows**.

In the water
Alligators and crocodiles make nests on riverbanks from mud and plants. The female lays her eggs in the middle where it is damp, then covers them up. She sits on top of the eggs to guard them. Turtles bury their eggs in nests deep in the sand to keep them safe and warm. When the baby turtles hatch, they race across the sand to the sea.

◀ When the female crocodile hears squeaking noises from the nest, she uncovers it and waits for the eggs to hatch.

▼ After hatching, turtles have to run quickly to reach the water safely. **Predators** such as crabs and raccoons lie in wait.

Quiz Corner

● How often do chimpanzees make their nests?

● Where do turtles dig their nests?

● How do alligators protect their eggs?

Overnight beds

Every night, the adult chimpanzee makes a sleeping nest high in a tree. First it bends down a few branches to make a mattress, then it covers the wood with soft leaves. A few more leaves make a pillow.

▼ The chimpanzee takes about five minutes to build its nest for the night.

The nest is large enough for young chimps to sleep alongside their mother.

Burrows and Tunnels

Most animals that live in **burrows** and tunnels have strong teeth or paws to help them dig through the soil. Some underground homes are no more than holes in the ground. Others, such as rabbit **warrens**, are made up of a network of tunnels that lead to areas for sleeping, living, and tending to their young.

CHATTERBOX

Wild gerbils shelter from the desert sun in deep underground burrows. There, it is cool enough for the gerbils to sleep. At night, the animals come out to search for food.

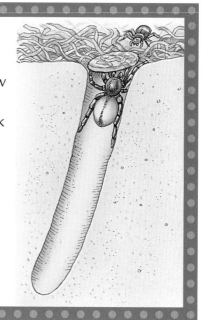

Setting a trap
The trapdoor spider's burrow is hidden by a lid made of silk and soil. The spider waits inside. When an insect passes by, the spider pulls it in and slams the door shut.

▼ At night, a mother mole may come to the surface to search for grass and leaves, which she will use to line her nest.

Mole holes
The mole spends most of its life underground, digging and guarding tunnels. It loosens the soil with its long snout, then digs through the soil with its spadelike paws, eating insects as it goes along. At the end of one tunnel, the mole will make a large room for sleeping. The mole will make another room for storing its favorite food—earthworms.

20

Escape!
European rabbits build their homes with special entrances called bolt holes. While feeding on the surface, they stay close to the bolt holes. In times of danger they rush down them and out of trouble.

Quiz Corner

- With what do animals dig?
- Why do wild gerbils spend the day underground?
- Where do trapdoor spiders lie in wait for their food?
- What is a mole's favorite food?

▼ In the early morning and evening, rabbits leave the safety of their warren to feed outside.

Look at: Burrows and Tunnels, page 20

Underground Towns

Prairie dogs are rabbit-sized **rodents** that live on the grasslands of the United States. Hundreds of prairie dogs live together in connected **burrows**, called towns. Each family has its own home in the town. Prairie dogs spend about half of their lives underground, only leaving their burrows to feed.

CHATTERBOX

Prairie dogs recognize each other by their smell. When two prairie dogs meet, they rub noses to find out if the other is a friend or not.

Living together

A prairie dog town has many tunnels and rooms. It may also have several entrance holes and escape hatches. These are loosely covered with soil and can be opened in a hurry. Often, rattlesnakes lurk in the tunnels. When a prairie dog smells a snake, it quickly blocks up the tunnel.

▼ Each burrow has rooms for different uses, such as sleeping and caring for young prairie dogs.

Standing guard

During the day, a few prairie dogs stand guard over the town, while others **graze**. When the guards spot an enemy, they bark a loud, shrill alarm call and the others dive into their burrows. The guards whistle when it is safe for them to come out again.

Prairie dogs keep watch for .... *enemies, such as eagles.*

Baby prairie dogs can leave the nest when they are six weeks old.

Towns in danger

Prairie dog towns used to be much bigger than they are today. One town in Texas was home to about 400 million prairie dogs. It was about the size of Ireland! Today, many prairie dogs have been killed by farmers who want to use the grasslands for growing crops or for grazing cattle.

▲ Burrowing owls nest in prairie dog towns. The burrows are not always safe, because prairie dogs often steal owl eggs.

Prairie dogs pile mounds of soil around each entrance hole to keep the rain out and to let fresh air in.

Quiz Corner

- In which country do prairie dogs live?

- Why do farmers kill prairie dogs?

- What other animal sometimes lives in prairie dog burrows?

If a burrow becomes overcrowded, the parents leave their young in the old burrow and make a new home for themselves.

Look at: Beaver Lodges, page 8; Mobile Homes, page 26

Underwater Homes

There are plenty of places for animals to live underwater, among clumps of water plants, or in the dark nooks and crannies of rocks and coral reefs. Many underwater animals make their homes in soft sand or mud on the seabed, while others live in, or on, other creatures.

Sharing a home

The clown fish lives safely among the stinging arms of the sea anemone. Amazingly, the clown fish does not get stung. Its skin is covered in a thick slime that protects it. **Predators** are stung by the anemone if they come too close to the clown fish.

SEE FOR YOURSELF

Make an underwater viewer by cutting off both ends of a clear plastic bottle. Cover one end and the sides with a sheet of food wrap, making sure water cannot seep in. Secure with a rubber band. Now you can look beneath the surface of ponds and rock pools.

▼ Clown fish help to keep sea anemones clean by removing dirt and waste.

What a mouthful

Most fish do not have permanent homes, but a few make homes for their young for a short time. The mouthbreeder keeps its eggs tucked inside its mouth for about ten days, until the eggs hatch. The young stay close to the parent for a few days, then swim away.

▲ The entrance to an octopus's home is usually well hidden and just big enough for the octopus to squeeze through.

▲ At the first sign of danger, newly hatched mouthbreeders dart back into their mother's mouth.

Places to hide

Rocks make safe hiding places for a variety of sea creatures. A few, such as the purple sea urchin, drill into rocks to make their homes. Others, such as octopuses, seek out rock crevices or cracks in coral reefs. Some female octopuses even clean their dens before they lay their eggs there.

Quiz Corner

● What protects the clown fish from the sting of the sea anemone?

● Where does the mouthbreeder keep its eggs?

● Which animal drills into rock to make its home?

Look at: Underwater Homes, page 24

Mobile Homes

Animals such as snails and crabs do not leave their homes behind when they look for food. Instead, they take their homes with them for protection. Other animals keep their young safe by carrying them around.

Baby carriers

Kangaroos and koalas are **marsupials**. A mother marsupial feeds her baby milk from inside her pouch. The baby, called a joey, lives inside the pouch until it is about nine months old.

▼ In the grasslands of Australia, kangaroos hop along with their joeys, feeding on plants.

CHATTERBOX

The shaggy fur of the sloth is the perfect nesting site for one type of moth. The moth lays her eggs in the fur. When the eggs hatch into caterpillars, they eat tiny plants, called algae, that also grow in the sloth's fur.

A joey keeps close to its mother. When danger threatens, it hops back into her pouch.

Solid armor

The tortoise has a shell that is attached to its body. The shell grows as the animal grows. When a tortoise is in danger, it can pull itself all the way inside the shell. Most crabs also have shells that protect their soft bodies. The hermit crab does not have its own shell, but it uses an old whelk or cockleshell. When the hermit crab grows too big for this shell, it finds another one.

 The hermit crab tightly grips its borrowed shell to keep the shell in place.

▲ The shell of this giant tortoise is made of layers of tough horn and bone.

Quiz Corner

● Name three types of animals that have shells to protect their bodies.

● What do hermit crabs use as a home?

● On which animal's fur do some moths lay their eggs?

Look at: Underground Towns, page 22

Living with People

Did you know that you share your home with all sorts of animals? Tiny **mites**, moths, and beetles live under the floorboards and in soft furnishings. Birds may nest under the roof or even in the chimney. All over your home, there are places for animals to hide and food for them to eat.

▶ Many people keep animals in their home. In return for food and a cozy bed, pets give us love and friendship.

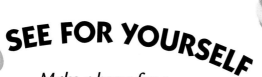 **SEE FOR YOURSELF**

Make a home for a bat or bird by putting up a birdhouse in your yard. Ask an adult to help you. The house will be a safe place in which birds or bats can shelter.

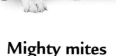

Mighty mites
Dust mites live in most peoples' homes, though the mites are too small to see. They live on household dust, and their favorite spot is your bed! Some people are **allergic** to mites, which make them sneeze.

In the yard
For animals, city or suburban yards are like patches of countryside. They attract all sorts of animals. Grass snakes and toads live under piles of wood and leaves, and squirrels build dreys in trees. Foxes and raccoons raid trash cans for food.

Homes under threat

All over the world, animal homes are being destroyed to make room for farms, roads, and buildings. These animals have to look for new places to live. Many move to cities or towns, where they find warmth, food, and shelter.

▼ Some animals find it easy to live in new surroundings. They use garbage that people leave behind.

Quiz Corner

● What creatures might be living in your home?

● Why do animals move to towns and cities?

● Where is the dust mite's favorite home?

Grass snakes enjoy basking on warm surfaces.

Spiders can spin their webs almost anywhere.

Seat stuffing makes a perfect bed for field mice.

Birds look for sheltered places to build their nests.

Amazing Facts

● Beaver **dams** are usually about 75 feet long. The biggest ever was built across the Jefferson River in Montana. It was almost half a mile long and strong enough for a person to ride across on horseback.

☆ *Some birds do not bother to build their own nests. The European cuckoo lays its egg in other birds' nests. Then it leaves its chick to be looked after by the new parent.*

● While a caddisfly **larva** turns into an adult, it lives underwater inside a case made of grains of sand, twigs, plant stems, and pieces of shell. This protects its soft body and makes it difficult for hungry fish to swallow. Its home is known as a log cabin.

☆ *Parrot fish live on coral reefs. By day, they swim about the reef, eating pieces of coral. At night, they build a jellylike sleeping bag around their bodies. This helps to protect them as they sleep. The sleeping bag takes about half an hour to build.*

☆ *Pencil-thin pearlfish have strange homes. They live inside the bodies of sluglike creatures called sea cucumbers. Two or three fish spend the day asleep inside a sea cucumber with their heads poking out of its tail end.*

● The **larvae** of petroleum flies live in California in pools of sticky oil. They feed on other tiny insects that get trapped in the oil. The larvae breathe through tubes that reach up to the surface like snorkels.

☆ *Some birds use unusual materials to build their nests. A stork's nest in France contained several pairs of stockings, fur caps, shoes, and buttons. A pair of crows in India made their nest from gold eyeglass frames, which they stole from a nearby shop.*

● In South Africa, sociable weaver birds build huge umbrella-shaped nests and divide them into rooms. Each nest may have up to ninety-five rooms, with a pair of birds in each room.

Glossary

allergic An unpleasant reaction; such as sneezing, coughing or itching, to dust, pollen, insect stings or food.

breeding Mating to produce young of one's kind.

burrows Holes in the ground that animals use as homes.

dam A barrier built across a river to hold back the water.

energy What gives things the power to move and grow.

fungus A living thing similar to a plant but having no leaves. A mushroom is a fungus.

graze To eat grass.

herd A large group of similar animals that feeds or lives together.

hexagons Shapes with six sides, all the same length.

honeycomb A sheet of wax cells made by bees. Many honeycombs make up a hive.

larva The baby stage of an insect. A larva may also be called a grub. *Larvae* is the word for more than one *larva*.

mammals Animals that give birth to live young and feed them with the mother's milk.

marsupial A **mammal** whose young are fed

in a pouch on the mother's body.

mites Tiny eight-legged creatures.

nurseries Places where baby animals are born or cared for.

pollen A yellow powder produced by flowers and collected by bees. Bees use pollen for food.

predators Animals that hunt and kill other animals for food.

rodents A group of **mammals** with gnawing teeth. Mice, rabbits, and squirrels are rodents.

warren A rabbit's underground home.

Index

Published in the USA by
C.D. Stampley Enterprises, Inc.,
Charlotte, NC, USA.
Created by Two-Can Publishing Ltd.,
London. English language edition
© Two-Can Publishing Ltd., 1997

Managing Editor: Christine Morley
Commissioning Editor: Robert Sved
Art Director: Carole Orbell
Senior Designer: Gareth Dobson
Picture research: Laura Cartwright
Consultant: Sandi Bain
Production: Adam Wilde
Additional Research: Inga Phipps
Artwork: Bill Donohoe, Teri Gower,
Peter Bull, Mel Pickering and Dai Owen

ISBN 1-58087-002-3

Photographic credits: front cover:
Planet Earth Pictures; p. 4: Planet
Earth Pictures; p. 5: Frank Lane
Picture Agency; p. 6: Robert Harding;
p. 8: Oxford Scientific Films;
pp. 10/11(c): Bruce Coleman Ltd;
p. 11: Frank Lane Picture Agency;
p. 12: BBC Natural History Unit;
p. 14: Ardea London Ltd; p. 16: Frank
Lane Picture Agency; p. 17: Bruce
Coleman Ltd; p. 18(t): Ardea London
Ltd, (b) Zefa; pp. 19/20/21: Bruce
Coleman Ltd; p. 23: BBC Natural
History Unit; p. 25: Oxford Scientific
Films; p. 27(l): Bruce Coleman Ltd,
(r): Frank Lane Picture Agency Ltd;
p. 28: John Englefield.